Setting Up Shop

Low Cost Marketing Strategies for Independent Retail Stores

Jane Webster

The Butler Publishing Group

ISBN-10: 1448665744
ISBN-13: 9781448665747

Printed in the United States of America.

Contents

1

The Retail Slump

The weak economy has taught us all some serious lessons about what customers are *really* looking for. These lessons have demanded some serious adjustments in how we do business—the way we evaluate our business, the way we market our business, and the way we conduct our business.

And, of course, everything costs a lot more money. Retail is failing left and right, and anybody that isn't a chain retailer has twice as much of a challenge ahead of them in terms of attracting and keeping business. Especially since the retail slump isn't entirely about the economy—it's also about the internet. Retailers have got to work harder than ever to compete with the in-home shopping experience.

What the Weak Economy has taught us

The weak economy has taught us the actual factors behind customer loyalty and the force that drives sales. It was a factor that we were able to ignore when things were good, because there was enough luck and enough money flowing freely during the boom that we hardly noticed the factor at all. In fact that factor was so misunderstood that we allowed things to get more and more impersonal.

What was the factor? Quite simply it was our ability to form a relationship with our customers and target a specific audience. It was also our ability to create the right experience for those customers in that target market. When things were good impulse sales could drive a great deal of business on top of our regular customers and reoccurring sales. Now everything is different, those relationships are all we have left.

Those retailers who never forgot are certainly having less of a problem surviving the slump than the retailers that are having to play catch up.

So now you have no choice—you've got to establish relationships with your customers. You've got to create a marketing experience that lets people know that they are going to find that relationship when they come in the door. For your target audience, you have no choice but to create a siren's call that lets your customers know that *your* store is created just for *them*.

Very little else is going to get them away from their computers and their living rooms, where they can buy nearly anything they want on Amazon or eBay. Of course, you can put an internet store front together and make some sales that way—but you still have to have enough of a name and enough of a relationship to take your customers to the internet store front in the first place!

Customer loyalty runs off the exact opposite factors from the factors we'd always assumed. For the longest time we believed that loyalty was driven by special offers, points, sales, discounts, and gimmicks. Turns out customer service with a smile, competence, a great product, a pleasant experience and being greeted by name wherever possible rank much higher on the list of reasons why customers stay loyal to a merchant than any amount of points and gimmicks.

In point of fact, customers don't even tend to use the loyalty points and the gimmicks. The cards and programs end up forgotten at the bottom of drawers. So if you've been trying to shore up your store by cutting prices, creating programs, passing out gifts and kicking up the hype it's time to turn your business around!

Believe it or not being personable alone can do a great deal to seize the edge over your competition. In a world of automated menus people are appreciative of personal care. Seem counterintuitive in a world where you're competing with the internet? At least the internet is quick when it's busy being impersonal.

Customers want an experience that's built just for them, so the foundation of everything else you're going to do is going to revolve firmly around defining your target audience. You really aren't trying to sell to everyone on the planet. You're trying to sell a specific group of people with a specific series of needs. You might sell one or two others of course—there's always impulse buys—but you're building your store around that target audience. It's not just your USP anymore, it's also your UTC—your unique targeted customer.

When you think of your UTC you shouldn't try to think in terms of faceless demographics. It's not about age, gender, economic range and living area. That's all faceless information.

It's about the maternity store that's serving Cathy, a 28 year old new mom who is still young enough to be hip, dedicated to her career, and needs clothes that honor all of this at the same time that she transitions into motherhood. She doesn't want ugly old fashioned maternity clothes—she wants an experience that still leaves her feeling sexy, cool, and competent.

Personalizing your ideal customer can help you decide how to appeal to her. It can tell you how to lay out your store, how to put together a window display, and the way you're going to create your advertisement campaign to appeal to this woman. It doesn't matter that Cathy is a fictional construct—you know that there are enough women *like* Cathy in your city. You are looking for Cathy and all of the women like her. You're working hard to appeal to her, your UTC.

Your UTC is not necessarily someone fictional—you might know a real customer who embodies everybody you're trying to serve right now. You should still write down a short paragraph about him or her now, something that helps you visualize exactly who your customers are. Remember you've got to get past all those impersonal details to truly understand this exercise.

Even doing this exercise can help to create a shift in your mindset that your customers will sense. You want the people who walk into your store to understand that they are not demographics in your store. They are not prospects. They are people, and you're going to change everything around until these people come first.

Here's the thing—everything has had to become less "salesy." The traditional sales and marketing model has become more and more ineffective simply because more and more people are tuning it out. This was starting to be true even before the bottom fell out of the economy. Now, as people hold to their purse strings just a bit tighter and scrutinize every purchase the principle is holding true to an even greater extent. When people stop to evaluate whether or not they are going to spend money with a merchant—any merchant—now they are looking for every possible reason to say "no" to the purchase. Those internal "filters" that have always helped customers make decisions have been raised even higher than they were before. Those "walls" that a customer had always put up between you and them are thicker and wider.

It's no longer appropriate nor even largely possible to push a customer through your door. Instead these customers have to be gently coaxed inside. They can't be pushed or convinced to the cash register. They have to be quietly persuaded that the trip to the cash register is in their best interests. It's no longer enough to match a product or a service to a need—you have to be able to prove that you care about the customer too. It can be a daunting prospect for anyone who is trained in the more traditional mindsets.

Because this is the case, when it comes to the sales side of things it's often more important to train your staff to take care of your customer with a smile on their face than it is to teach them the latest "selling techniques." Your marketing aim is often far more involved with creating a welcoming atmosphere than it is involved with trying to manipulate people into working with you.

It's possible to have more than one UTC. You might have 3-4 different sorts of "categories" of customers that come through your door. This happens most often when you have a larger store that appeals to a variety of people. You might have an appeal to both professional women and professional men looking for suits, for example. You might appeal to several different age ranges or life stages. That's fine. Write down each UTC as if they were a unique, individual person. Name them. When you see someone come into the store decide which of your named UTCs your customers are "brothers" or "sisters" to.

Having multiple UTCs can complicate everything from advertising to merchandising, but you have to know where you stand. If you do have multiple UTCs you might need to run multiple ads and set up your store in such a way as to appeal to all of them. Or you might just need to devote a few smaller sections of your store to a few of the UTCs while focusing on your one, backbone, "Bread and Butter" UTC. If 47% of your custom comes from one particular UTC and you have identified 3 other UTCs that divide the rest of the custom between them then you're still going to aim, laser-like, primarily at that first UTC.

The New Consumer Mindset

Whether you want to blame the internet or a simple lack of patience for the new consumer mindset is completely up to you. You can also blame a certain anger on the part of the customer who has been subjected to a long list of bad service, bad deals, hidden fees, bad products, and bad promises. Customers are not about to take anything you have to offer on faith anymore. They want value for their money and what's more, they want you to prove it.

Brick and mortar retailers have some challenges in that area. Where the internet marketer is free to slap up some great content and use it to position himself or herself as an expert, you've got a storefront to run. Informational brochures on your product are all fine and good but you and I both know that the consumer who is physically walking into a store is measuring value, suddenly, by a whole different set of parameters.

That said, the measuring stick is there—it's always there. In the retail environment the value gets measured on the way the staff acts. It gets measured by the way the store looks, the product the store carries, and how attentive the store is to the needs and wants of the customer. That UTC comes into play firmly here, because the targeted customer is going to sense, on a very subconscious level, that total attention to his or her needs. What's more, the customer who does not quite fall into that target market but who might still want something your store has to offer can sense the effort on your part as well. Each type of customer will respond.

That's why many of the marketing methods we're going to discuss really will be low cost or cost effective strategies, because they don't always rely on money at all. It's the spirit behind the form that matters as much as the form itself ever did. It's the attitude behind the medium that carries through and turns the customer on or off. If you don't believe the customer is capable of sensing both you are absolutely out of your mind.

You've likely been trained to run everything you do on hard factors like cost effectiveness, conversion, and the bottom line. Today's customer demands the soft factors. Are you personable? Do you care about them? Do you take an interest in them? Have you done everything you can to make their shopping experience smooth, easy, convenient, and fun?

Are You Personable? Being personable is locked up in two places. The atmosphere of your store is one of them— your store should feel welcoming and pleasant, *especially* to that unique targeted customer. It should have a clean, open layout and a sparkling feel. It should have warm comfortable lighting and a good temperature. The air should not be stuffy, dusty, or stifling. The paging system should not be going off constantly or in an annoying fashion. The music, if there is any at all, should be chosen with the targeted customer in mind and played at a volume that does not detract from the customer's shopping experience.

The other half of this equation comes in the form of staff training. Does your staff greet the customer when the customer walks into your store? Has the staff been trained to recognize and appeal to the different types of personalities that walk inside of the store? For example, a more gregarious person will want to engage in conversation with your staffers where a snap decision maker might just want to get in, get out, and get back to business.

Does the staff smile? Do they act like they are there to serve the customer or is the customer an unbearable interruption? Do they answer customer questions thoroughly and helpfully? When the customer asks where something is do they vaguely point out an aisle or do they walk the customer there themselves? When the store gets busy is there an air of energy and fun or is there an air that the staff has been frazzled and harassed? When customer service problems pop up does each staffer have the ability to "own" the problem and make decisions to fix it (within guidelines) or is there a complicated chain of command that forces the customer to wait while the associate consults someone higher up the food chain?

Are simple matters like straightening up displays, picking up garbage, and ringing up customers treated as someone else's job or problem or are they a part of everybody's job description? When the customer calls on the phone is he placed on hold for a long time or are his questions answered immediately?

The Retail Slump

Do the associates speak in friendly tones? Do they seem bored or engaged? Are the associates themselves happy? Happy associates are more likely to create the kind of atmosphere that creates happy customers, so you should consider going ahead and letting the associates, if any, talk to you about their needs. For example if their feet get tired because they are forced to stand all day then you might consider a stool for the register. It's not going to hurt your business any. If they aren't making enough money with you to pay their bills they'll be resenting you, resenting the customers, and quite possibly trying to decide what they can steal from you to even the score. Counterintuitive as it may be in the rough economy a pay raise coupled with new training might go far in ensuring loyalty out of your staff, which in turn ensures your customers are treated right.

Do you have a firm store culture that can be expressed through any kind of training or orientation session? Did you know that employees who receive an orientation session that discusses the vision and the culture of the company are very likely to stay loyal and happy? They want to carry out that vision—if that vision is a positive one that truly takes care of the people who walk through your door.

Here's where you lose the game of being personable: when your staff and your customers both have a feeling that you are only out for yourself. When your staff gets that feeling they pass it to your customers. When your customers get that feeling they take it out on the staff, which stresses them out and breeds resentment. It's a never-ending cycle. Ironically, selfishness and greed, once the watchword of most business strategies, are traits which are likely to kill your business today if they aren't held in check.

Do you care about the customer and take an interest in him? What is the customer to you really? Are they people who walk through your door—people with real personalities, real lives, and real needs? Or are they walking wallets?

Answering this question may take some soul searching because none of us really would like to think of ourselves as the type of people who might treat a customer as a walking wallet. Yet look at the way many businesses are structured and you'll see the mindset everywhere. If you happened to slip into it somewhere along the way it is probably only because the predominant business culture supported that emotional mindset for a long, long time.

In fact, you might be having a hard time creating your UTC statement simply because you've never stopped to have any conversation with any customer that was not, in some form or fashion, either a sales conversation or the ubiquitous "customer service" conversation in which you were dealing with an infuriated sheep in wolf's clothing. Either of these two interactions can color your perception of the customer in a very negative or "walking wallet" style of light that is not really conducive to a feeling of caring towards them.

The only real remedy for this is to get down into your store if you don't do so already. Then you have to discipline yourself to have some conversations with your customers—conversations that revolve around getting to know them, and not sales or customer service.

If all of this seems like a useless exercise remember that you're laying the ground work for bigger things here. This is the new market research, as vital as researching competitors, more valuable than a dozen surveys. Nobody can deny that for some of us, it can be a strange, awkward exercise. You're used to thinking of these people as someone who you want something out of. You're now having to turn around, face that problem, admit to that problem, and make a conscious shift.

Nobody ever promised that the new economy would be easy. That said, when the shift is made you may come to like your work a lot more than you do now.

That's not to say these conversations can't have a bit more direct purpose later down the line. Every bit of information you know about your customer's world helps you to get closer to that person's reality. That person's reality is what determines his or her needs—and ultimately you'll be in a better position to match your product or service to the customer because you have a better understanding of *who he is.*

Where once you might have trained your associates to convince your customers and meet their objections, you'll now train them to work towards getting to the truth of that customer's situation. You'll train them to care about these people as individuals—and you'll watch your whole business shift as a result.

Have you done everything you can to make their shopping experience smooth, easy, convenient, and fun? Some establishments make their customers jump through so many hoops that it's certain they mistake them for trick circus ponies. A customer who tries for an exchange, return, or refund must prove their case before what amounts to a sort of magistrate's tribunal. Product is regularly moved, rearranged, and hidden to the point where customers have an enormous amount of trouble locating it. Some retailers don't hire enough staff at the counter and this results in long lines, back-ups, and issues.

Setting Up Shop

When you start walking around your store with your customer's mind on you will easily pick out these problems and issues. You can also consider employing the use of store "shopping" services that will give you an unbiased customer's eye view of the experience that your shop creates.

Again, much of the "fixes" are going to be counter-intuitive. While other shops are cutting associate hours, for example, you might have to consider expanding them so that you'll have enough people staffing the various areas of the store to make a difference when crowds are lining up.

For that matter, it might be simple aesthetics that need to change. Changing the decor of your shop to brighten up, update, or create a more professional or cohesive look and feel can go a long way towards altering consumer perception. A simple color change can be the difference between your customers finding your shop a fun place to be and finding it a difficult place to be.

It is only after you have made all of these evaluations and determinations that you're actually ready to tackle the task of marketing anything at all to the customer in any kind of a meaningful fashion. This is groundwork you're laying, groundwork of understanding. Of course—if you want a true customer's eye view, go to the customer. Now—the customer might not be completely honest with you. Nobody wants to hurt your feelings and this means you might not get accurate data.

You might have to employ someone who seems like a perfect stranger to ask your customers how they feel about your shop. Sometimes comment cards and simply sending out surveys is good, but often it doesn't entirely work for the simple enough reason that people don't take the time to fill them out. Again, too, people will tend to phrase things in the best positive light unless they're truly unhappy.

By contrast, they'll tell another consumer an awful lot of information they'll never give you. You can try to guess at the customer experience. You can try to ask people in to simulate the customer experience—but if those people are tied to you or your store in any way then they will not really be able to give you an unbiased look. You need the customer's opinion out of the customer's own mouth.

If your sales haven't slumped you're already doing something right, but the customer's opinion is more than likely showing up somewhere in the vicinity of the cash register. So don't delude yourself into thinking all is well. Unless sales are on the rise or hanging steady during this economic downturn, it's time to make some changes.

Then again you could find out that your customer is 100% happy with the entire experience—it's just that not enough people know about you to make up for layoffs, lost jobs, and rising bills. Customers who'd love to shop and stay loyal to you might not be able to. Marketing is the only thing you can turn to in order to stem a growing tide of customer attrition.

2

Store Layout

You've stopped to decide who your UTC is and you're ready to start moving on the improvements that will help your store not only survive, but thrive in this economic slump. You not only need a store that maximizes sales, but you also need a store which minimizes loss.

Store layout is all part of creating that clean, convenient, easy and fun store that your target is looking for. Even a man who loudly says he hates shopping is out to have fun when he visits his local fishing shop. You've got to create the store that appeals to that person you described when you wrote out who you were really trying to sell to.

You're not only trying to get a handle on the store layout— you know that you also need to get a handle on your best possible displays. Displays help draw customer's attention to product they might never have noticed otherwise, and whether you're trying to maximize impulse buys or simply to help the customer find the products and services that will serve him or her the most, it's worth putting some out.

Store Layout

Killer Displays

There's really a variety of reasons to use attractive product displays to your advantage. Displays can be used to:

- Ensure a product which is really going to benefit your customer gets the exposure it needs and deserves.

- Help maximize impulse buys on the part of the customer.

- Promote product that isn't moving fast enough.

- Announce any sort of sale or discount special that you have going on at your store.

- Announce any sort of seasonal promotion.

- Act as an in-store advertising front.

You have several different display methods at your disposal, and it's a good idea to familiarize yourself with all of them so that you can mix and match the best techniques for your business at any given time.

Point of purchase retail displays and in queue merchandising stands are two techniques that retailers are finding particularly effective in the current climate. Both of these are meant to maximize the impulse purchase. They also are meant to maximize your floor space—with only a limited amount of profit potential per square foot it's vital that you don't waste a thing. All the same you need to ensure you don't adopt a cluttered look, so these sorts of displays are perfect for achieving such ends.

Setting Up Shop

Point of purchase displays are placed right next to the checkout area. You've probably noted one every time you go to the grocery store—candy and pop are traditionally located right there at the conveyer belt and put right at child's eye level to help ensure that parents are subjected to childlike begging and pleading.

POP displays are getting a lot more sophisticated. Retailers are using creative electronic displays which can issue coupons on the spot, create digital pictures of the product to save space, and even allow customers to ask for more information right then and there. Since your associates can always go get a product for a customer you can save a lot of space by using one of these displays, as well as encourage more customer interaction with your staff.

Of course, such things may also be way out of your budget, forcing you to get creative with far more traditional means. A colorful box display containing quite a bit of the product you're trying to sell or even a large rack or poster displaying the product can certainly be equally effective to a high tech display—and even, perhaps, far more in line with your UTC and his or her experience. When you place shelving with product that you wish to move to either side of the customer on his or her way through the check out your POP display technically becomes an "In Queue" display.

The POP is certainly not the only place to build eye-catching displays that will suit your needs. Kiosks in the centre of the store, shelves at the end of shelves, and dynamic wall displays add to the customer's total shopping experience. They also help create a unique atmosphere in your store—something your particular UTC can't find anywhere else. That unique atmosphere is one of the things that will bring your customer to you again and again, so use it whenever and wherever you can.

Be sure and invest enough money in your displays as they will draw the eye before anything else inside of your store. Dissuading yourself of the notion that money spent on good displays and signage inside of the store is a waste is simply a matter of considering your reaction the last time you walked into a store and found a hand lettered poster on the wall to announce some sort of clearance sale. There are some things that look every bit as unprofessional as a dirty floor!

Next you must create your display in line with the generalized elements of a good display.

- Asymmetrical balance: the eye will pause at this form of balance where it will roam quite a bit more quickly over a symmetrically balanced display. This is a trifle counterintuitive as almost every bit of our mental and artistic schooling was taught to value and enjoy the aesthetic value of a fully symmetrical anything. After all the amount of symmetry people carry in their faces is one criteria we instinctively carry around to measure the concept of beauty. You do want a beautiful display but you also need a display that makes your customers stop what they're doing and pay attention to what *you've* gone and done.

- Colors should be bright, eye-catching and appropriate to the display. The display should look clean, crisp, and bright but it should also carry the overall feel and tone of the store with it so that it integrates seamlessly. A display that clashes with the feel of the store is just going to detract from the customer experience instead of add to it, and that will have the opposite effect from the one you are seeking.

- Each display should have a unique focal point, usually around the largest item on the display. The product, props, and signs should all come together at this focal point to create the impact that will move and sell your product. If at all possible your lighting should accent this focal point, almost haloing it so that the customer's eye is drawn, inevitably, towards your display.

- Clean lines—don't clutter up your display! If you add too many items you'll end up confusing your customer and tiring his eyes. Again, this is likely to have an effect that is 100% opposite of the effect you're actually seeking. If you're going to err, err on the side of less (but don't leave a naked display either).

You actually can hire display companies to help you create really professional, creative displays—but if you have to do it yourself these principles should help you. That said, if you do have to go "DIY" you should take the time to walk around other high street stores. Bring a notebook with you—whenever someone else's display really catches your eye, stop to mark down details. Where was the display? What kind of display was it? What product was on display? How did the merchant make use of color? How did the display add to (or detract from) the overall feel of the store?

Store Layout

With these notes you should be able to be able to sketch out a creative display that will serve you well. You may have to buy some additional materials (shelving, for example) or you may be able to use what's on hand.

Displays are also at their most effective when you are able to change them out on a regular basis. Displays need to be kept fresh or they will lose their effectiveness. As displays can be both time consuming and expensive, once a month is a fairly safe number when it comes to the length of time that you leave your display up before switching it out in favor of a new one.

Using Store Layout to Reduce Retail Shrink

Store layout is for the customers—mostly. Your sales will matter little if you lose a significant portion of your profits to theft. It may be that you need a new layout to remain competitive, and part of that will indeed be aimed at your UTC. However, if you've not been paying attention to shrink, now is the time to start.

Shrink—loss due to theft—generally comes from four sources. The most costly and frustrating source is usually employee theft. It's sad that we often have to protect ourselves against our own employees, but the statistics don't lie. 70% of retail employees will steal something from the store that employs them during their period of employment. Sometimes they will do this through some fairly creative means—price tag switching, discount abuse, and "Voiding" out purchases being popular theft choices.

The next biggest form of retail shrink is of course shoplifting, and while it's still an ugly problem it's certainly easier to stomach the idea of a stranger coming in to steal.

Setting Up Shop

This is certainly the first thing most people imagine when the subject of retail theft comes up.

A smaller percentage of "shrink" happens through simple human administrative error or vendor fraud, and neither of those are problems that you're going to solve by changing up your store layout.

The thing you're looking for here are blind spots. Shoplifters and even employees don't need but a few moments of unwatched time to perform a quick theft. Thieves also like areas with poor lighting. To maximize these defenses, take the time to look into the following measures:

- Arrange shelving in a manner that minimizes the opportunities for theft of every sort by keeping as much of the store as possible visible to the front cash register.

- Install lighting and mirrors which not only deter theft but make it easier for you or responsible, trustworthy employees to see what's going on in the store.

- Make sure the store is laid out so that customers have to pass the point of sale before they can leave the store.

- Though you should be doing this anyway, keeping the store neat and clean reduces many opportunities for theft. Disorder and confusion are breeding grounds for trouble!

Store Layout

- Create some displays with locking up the product in mind as well as selling it. Items like jewels, guns, watches, and weapons are already traditionally locked up in a glass case in many stores as it is. Besides, glass cases can make lovely merchandising displays.

There are certainly a variety of other loss prevention measures you can use of course. You can choose to install cameras. You can choose Sonitrol door scanners which seek out tagged product. You can find security guards and use signage which promises prosecution to anyone who tries to steal from you—all of these are effective.

However, you should think twice about employing them. In some stores these things will have a jarring effect on the customers. Some stores will integrate such methods seamlessly, without damaging their atmosphere or offending their customers. Other stores will manage instead to create a jarring, prisonlike effect that makes their target customers completely uncomfortable and destroys sales. You have to weigh the benefits against the potential losses, because even the best strategy in the world isn't going to get rid of all theft to begin with.

Besides, you don't have to resort to such overt tactics if you don't want to. You can integrate a great policy of customer service into your new store culture instead. Associates that roam the store, take the time to talk to each customer, and physically bring customers to the site of things they need to find remove opportunities for theft without even having to know that's what they're actively doing. Of course—it does help if they do know what they're doing, but remember that most thefts are "attacks of opportunity," so to speak. If you do everything in your power to remove as many opportunities as possible you will find you reduce your shrink rate while maintaining a high class atmosphere.

Big Store Layout Mistakes

Before you start making decisions about how to do your store layout right you should understand the biggest mistakes when it comes to store layout. In this way you'll be able to steer clear of the worst of the pitfalls. Remember this is a completely new economy and it's going to require new thought process on your part. You may need to come in on the day the store is typically closed just to create a new atmosphere. You may be committing some of these "layout deadly sins" already!

Using too much space. A good ad requires white space to relax the eye. A good store requires some unused space both to relax the eye and to just give customers the opportunity to *move* in your store. When you overdo it you create a cluttered, unpleasant, chaotic feel. It's almost the equivalent of invading your customer's "personal space" when the shelves seem to push in on them as if physically grabbing at them, perhaps in a misguided effort to force them to buy.

This is sometimes a retailer's biggest temptation simply because he has an awful lot of product that *he wants and needs to **move**.* So the unhappy retailer goes into a sort of panic mode and shoves as much of this overage at the customer as he possibly can. The sense of desperation fills the aisles to the point where the customer is all but herded out the door, empty handed. Even if no salesperson speaks to the customer at all they are left with the sensation that they have run some sort of gauntlet of obnoxious representatives shoving product at them left and right.

Store Layout

Any merchandising display you've done under these circumstances registers only as more clutter.

Lack of a clearly designated entrance. It's sometimes hard to tell if some stores are opened or closed. It's sometimes hard to tell the employee entrance from the customer entrance. While you'd think that customers would recognize the entrance facing the street as the correct entrance this isn't always the case. Your signs should always point clearly to the front door anyway—it's a psychological thing that helps ease the customer's mindset through the process of moving from the street to the door and ultimately to the interior of the store.

You should always go ahead and label exactly how to open the door too. You don't want to lose a frazzled, absent minded customer just because she pulled when she should have pushed and assumed the store was locked up and closed. It sounds absolutely ridiculous but *it happens*. Remember the lives of your customers: these people are, by and large, stressed out, busy people with a zillion distractions. Don't assume they get it. Just go ahead and make it easy on them. Everyone will feel better for it.

Bad lighting. Bad lighting makes your store look seedy or spooky. Good lighting makes your store look welcoming and attractive. Invest money in the proper lighting! Don't leave lights that flicker eerily overhead or are burnt out altogether, for example. Work with something other than luminescent lighting as well. You need accent lighting, which not only increases the light in the store but helps differentiate your lovely product displays.

It's true that nobody's going to walk into your store and say, "What lovely lighting! This makes my experience ever so much more interesting!" However, remember that the selling process happens at much under the surface thoughts as it does at the level of conscious thought. You can use a combination of fluorescent lights as well as metal-halogen lamps to achieve the desired effects.

Bad Fitting Rooms. If you have ever been in a dirty, cramped, and uninviting fitting room you instantly know what I'm talking about. Some fitting rooms are small, closet like spaces with slatted doors, for example, in which nobody could ever hope to put on a pair of pants without fear that they might tumble seat first to the floor, potentially with said pants tangled all about their legs for all to see (because there's only ¾ of a door to begin with). Confronted with such a space many customers will simply pass on your merchandise rather than risk the agony and humiliation.

You ought to also check the lighting in the fitting rooms as well. Fitting rooms should not be lit like a public bathroom, in which it is virtually impossible to look good in anything at all short of resorting to Hollywood levels of make-up. Any clothing retailer knows that looking and feeling good in the clothing is so crucial to the purchase decision that he will help the customer in any way possible to look and feel good in those clothes. If you wouldn't want to change in there then don't make your customers change in there either.

Craning necks and crouching knees. Some retailers place their merchandise so high that the customer not only has to back up half a dozen paces to *see* it, but they also have to hunt for some associate to get it with a giant hook to touch it or try it on. Since standing there waiting for the associate with the giant hook is a certified pain for most people nearly none of that merchandise will end up anywhere but the clearance rack some 3 months later. By the same token, any merchandise the customer has to kneel to get a good look is doomed to sell well under its full potential.

Store Layout

Don't put anything higher than about six feet or lower than about a foot and a half. This way you can avoid annoying your customers while making sure all of your merchandise is actually seen—a winning situation on both counts.

Failure to control smells. If you have a break room be sure that the smells from the break room aren't filtering out into the store. If at all possible send your employees to an outdoor area for their lunches and break. Imagine shopping for a high quality perfume only to be distracted by the pervasive smell of the garlic and onions from someone's Italian extravaganza.

This problem goes even deeper than unpleasantness. Some people are really quite sensitive to smells. Smells can cause some customers allergic reactions or painful migraines which are not at all going to put them into the buying mood—and might well create some unpleasant associations that keep the customer from coming back for good.

Maximizing Sales per Square Foot

Once the deadly layout sins are contained you can start turning your attention to your true goal when you do anything with your layout—maximizing the amount of money you receive per square foot of the building. After all, you're already looking at one of your major liabilities per square foot. Most retailers lease, and most leases are calculated on a dollar amount per square foot that the store takes up. Therefore if you're not daily making a much larger amount of money per square foot you're not only keeping yourself from paying your employees, but you're also not even managing to clear the rent for that day, which all amounts into a rather untenable long term situation.

This shift in mindset can help you escape some of the traps a great deal. Rather than thinking in terms of "moving this product" or "moving that product" you'll be asking yourself how you can make the most of your space to increase sales on the whole. The temptation to cram every square foot of space with merchandise should go away when you realize the negative impact it will have on SpSF. The hesitation you might have over purchasing still more lighting should disappear when you realize the positive potential impact on sales per square foot.

This method of measurement is really nothing new—it's a time honored method of measuring the productivity of any given retail site. That's because the store's productivity can be quite deceptive until the sales per square foot are factored into account. After all, $1000 worth of sales may look great until you realize that you're paying $1000 in rent each month for that site. Barely breaking even. Then again if you're paying $200 in rent for that site $1000 worth of sales starts to look like a much happier figure.

You can't include certain space in your calculations. The break room, stock room, and your office, for example, don't really factor into the equation. These areas are not expected to generate sales, so they're not used even if you're paying rent on them. The formula goes as follows:

Total Net Sales/Square Feet of Selling Space =SpSF.

Having figured out this number you've got to figure out how to increase it. Take photographs as you walk through your store so you can really evaluate every aspect of your store's appearance. You've already done the research with your customers, after all, so now it's time to really start circling off those areas that need improvement.

Store Layout

You also need to identify your hot products vs. your loser products. Clear out the losers and leave the hot products. I wholly understand your desire to sell these things but you might not want to use up a whole lot of space on filling up your clearance or sales racks. Either get rid of them in one big sweeping sale or throw them into your storehouse, cut your losses, forget about them and sell them separately on Craigslist later. The economy is too nasty to leave losers in your store just because you are angry that you have not recouped the losses of purchasing them yet.

Before you actually start making any changes in your store you should draw the store as it is and start making some drawings of the store as it *could* be. Mark out why you think these changes will help you increase your sales as randomly moving things about in the hopes that it will help won't necessarily leave you any farther ahead.
You should also take particular note of some of the most important places in your store. Pay attention to how you've been handling these in particular—and jot down any ideas you might have for how you can do better.

- The space right in front of the door, which is the transition point between the street and your store. This space has a job, and the job is to get the customer focused on your shopping.

- The fixtures just past this space. They're sometimes known as "Speed bumps" since you're hoping the customers will slow down and buy something.

- The first right turn in America or the first left turn anywhere else, simply because everyone shops the way they drive. Therefore you need to pay very special attention to that "road".

- The first wall your shoppers see, because it helps to form the first impression of your store.

- The checkout counter! Though this zone is on the customer's way *out* it colors the entire memory that the customer will have about your store. It'll color whether your customer decides to return and become a regular as well. Is it cramped? Did you stock items that the customer might need out of consideration for him or her?

Basic Floor plans

Visit http://tinyurl.com/ng9m43/. Here, you will see a series of potential floor plans. They are meant simply to give you a visual representation of different things you might do with your store floor plan.

With all of these different options you're now in a position to try to decide what the best floor plan for the job is. While many people will try to give you hard and fast rules, there is in fact only one rule:

What will make the best shopping experience for your unique, targeted customer? If the floor plan would not be soothing and interesting to your customer then there is **absolutely no point in using it.**

These floor plans are frameworks anyway—ideas that you can hang your ultimate store design upon. You also, of course, have the ultimate option of hiring a professional store planner to help you out, but just in case you can't this creativity will fall on you. Use graph paper to map out the actual dimensions of your store, plan out merchandise, and alter problem areas. You can even turn this entire affair into a promotional event by posting the potential layouts in your store and asking customers to vote!

Once you've chosen your new layout you should stick with it if at all possible. Customers might forgive one new store layout in order to "better serve their needs," (and make them more prone to shop, but you don't have to tell them that) but they're not going to be too forgiving if they find a different layout every time they enter the store. In point of fact customers rarely enjoy too much change if they like the store they're standing in. Change your layout only if you feel like it's not working very well for your UTC or creating the image that you want it to create. Don't let the customers back into the new layout until you're very sure that you know it is right and you intend to leave it alone. Otherwise your customers will get exasperated and frustrated. Many times people go into their favorite stores, subconsciously, because they know they'll find exactly what they need when they need it, and moreover they'll know *where to find it* in time for them to get back to the office before their official lunch break ends. If you rob them of this experience you're going to be asking for a fair amount of trouble—or at least you're going to miss out on all those lunch-runner buyers that are so helpful to your bottom line.

3

Window Displays

Apartment managers go for "curb appeal" when they try to sell their properties to potential tenants. You have your own form of curb appeal—the window display. The window display achieves several ends at once. It serves as an advertisement that uses space you already have available to you. It helps tease the customer and lure them into the store.

Your ultimate goal with a window display is an attempt to move the driver from the street to your front door. It has to grab attention, appeal to the target customer, and create appeal. This is not easy—it's enough of an art form that there are professional retail window dressers available on the market should you have the money to hire such a professional. If you do not, you'll have to tackle this task all on your own.

Generating Walk-In Traffic

Did you know that a really good window display can bring in as many customers as an expensive TV ad? That's how vital this process is. So you're not just tossing some merchandise into a window and hoping for the best here. You're going to use your display as a form of advertising, something which helps the customer size up, in the space of a couple of seconds, who your store is and what it's all about. It's in the space of those few seconds that the customer will decide whether to walk into your store or not.

So a window display needs to be creative and uncluttered. It may even need to make use of more senses than sight. You can make use of sound and even, in some limited cases, smell to bring people inside of your shop. Your display cannot be random or haphazard—it has to be a cohesive message around a centralized theme to get the point across. Colors, shapes, lighting and a sense of cohesion with all of the other displays in your store are all keys to the success of the project.

You also, of course, need to stand out from all the other window displays on your street. Your window display has to reach out and grab people who have walked by a dozen other shops. Here is your opportunity to make a great first impression.

Many clothiers of course use mannequins to create window displays, but beware. A group of mannequins just standing there doesn't always get the job done. After all, dozens of shops have dressed up life sized dolls in them, staring blankly out at the rest of the world as they pass by.

Mannequins seeming to *do* something, however, can attract a lot of attention. If you're doing a summer line then mannequins standing in beach sand playing volleyball in the new summer line invokes an image. It helps to create a picture in the customer's mind of doing that very fun thing. It reminds the customer that she, has some beach going and volleyball playing of her own this season and might entice her inside simply because the vision is there. Mannequins standing in neat rows in bathing suits won't create that picture—they'll just register as bathing suits. It'll take the word "bathing suit" a bit too long to travel through the synapses to create such a picture for the customers.

Putting up a small banner or sign that asks a question and creates a call to action can help seal the deal. For example:

Ready for summer fun yet? Come in!

With the picture sealed and created in the customer's mind most people will go ahead and step inside. In other words you've set the stage—you've managed to create the circumstances that entice the customer to come inside.

What if you don't use mannequins because you don't sell clothes? What if you just have new televisions? Should you just stack and pyramid a bunch of new televisions? Or would it be more effective to go ahead and get out that HD big screen and set it in the front window and use some mannequins to simulate a businessman flopping down into the couch at the end of the long day. You can use the television screen to create that sign or call to action that brings things inside.

Do you sell food of any sort? What about a display that makes the smell of your fresh baked bread waft right under the customer's nose while they look at your newest loaves of sourdough, all neatly arranged on a single blue plate on a slightly tilted table and placed in an otherwise dark window under a spotlight? What if just a bit of music— perhaps choirs of angels—played very softly on an external speaker so that you create the effect of a light from heaven coming down to show off this bread? Perhaps at the base of the table you can spoof off those billboards, using a small black and white sign that says:

Come in and try the bread.

-God.

Your creativity and attention to detail will say something about your store. It will help set you apart from the competition and it will demand participation in what your store has to offer.

Of course, one of the reasons we covered your store layout first is because your window display won't do much for you if the interior of the store doesn't live up to the expectations your window display set. You should always move to make the experience cohesive. If you've used creativity and excitement in your window display then people are going to expect creativity and excitement when they walk through the door as well.

Sometimes selecting that central theme is the hardest part. Without that theme your display is sunk before it has begun. The theme can be an experience, a color scheme, or a holiday, but there has to be one. Start brainstorming some themes that you can use for your products and your store. Always keep your UTC in mind.

When in doubt go for simple displays, because they will look professional. Remember you really don't have all that much time to hold the customer's attention. Going for something simple and slick that the customer will remember is going to take you a lot farther than packing your window full of too many details. Obviously every product in your store is wonderful, but you really only have time to showcase a few of them in the window display.

Sometimes your window will get dirty, so replace any items that get dirty and make sure to clean up the window display regularly. When you've put your display into place stand outside of the display to see what it really looks like. Make any adjustments you need to make in order to make the display look perfect—you don't get a lot of opportunities this good and you want to make the most of this one.

Color can mean a lot. There is a message and an emotion that happens with colors.

White on its own brings very cold, clinical things to mind, so combine white with other colors as an eye catching contrast.

- Yellow is a cheerful, happy color that can invoke carefree feelings.

- Darker blues are soothing and make good backdrops. Lighter blues give that "ocean" feel which can be great for invoking the feelings of vacations and relaxation.

- Browns and tans are subdued, elegant colors that can bring the sensation of wealth and worth to a display—but be careful. Done incorrectly these colors can also just make your display look drab and boring.

Window Displays

- Black is another elegant, sophisticated color—it can also create a bold, hip feel. All by itself, though, it's dark, depressing, and too stark! Like white, black can make a fine contrast color.

- Red creates a sense of urgency—too much of it can be too aggressive and hard on the eye. It can also create a sensation of excitement, however.

- Orange is an earth shade which is good for conveying environmental friendliness, excitement, and a feeling of autumn.

- Purple is dramatic and can be associated with nobility and wealth—but be wary because some people find purple very tacky. The shade of purple definitely matters.

Window displays have to stay fresh to be effective. Some people suggest shifting your designs out every few *days*, but that's not terribly cost effective. In truth, once every month or once every three weeks is plenty. Themed, seasonal window displays are some of the easiest ways to go ahead and get people in the door, as people have needs for every season and holiday. Consider a window display for each of the following (American holidays, adjust if you're in another country):

- New Years (December 26—January 1)

- Winter Window Display #1 (January 1—February 1)

- Valentine's Day Display (February 2—February 14)

Setting Up Shop

- Spring Window Display #1 (February 15—March 3)

- St. Patrick's Day (March 4—March 17)

- Easter (March 17—Easter Monday)

- Spring Window Display #2 (Easter Monday—May 1)

- Mother's Day (May 2—Mother's Day)

- Summer Window Display #1 (Mother's Day—June 1)

- Father's Day Display (June 2—Father's Day)

- Summer Window Display #2 (Father's Day—August 1)

- Back-to-School Window Display (August 2—Labour Day)

- Fall Window Display #1 (Labor Day—October 15)

- Halloween Window Display (October 16—October 31st)

- Thanksgiving Window Display (November 1—Thanksgiving)

- Christmas Window Display (Black Friday—Christmas)

Window Displays

Obviously you are going to have to adjust these for your customers. A high end clothier or jeweler who caters to wealthy women in their fifties and sixties is not going to bother with a back-to-school display. A retail store who sells African themed clothing primarily to a black population might want to focus on Kwanza a lot harder then they'll want to focus on Christmas. Any store in Louisiana that misses the opportunity to do a Mardi Gras display is going to be out of synch with the rest of the state.

Taking the time to create your own window display calendar will not only make sure that you're not floundering for a theme when the time comes but it will also keep you disciplined and on track as far as switching out the displays goes. You might also work in other opportunities, such as the launch of a hot new product line that you really want to promote.

Finding the Best People to Work With

Working with local art and design students is one low cost way to get the best window displays without spending your entire advertising budget all in one place. Such people are often grateful for the experience and the portfolios, and they have the visual and artistic skills to help you. Theatre set designers will also have many of the skills in dramatic lighting that you might need.

You may need the help simply because window displays on the whole have gotten a lot more sophisticated over the years. Your simpler displays might not compete. If you're on a street with an awful lot of savvy, talented retailers then it won't do to simply struggle along on your own.

Setting Up Shop

Believe it or not your vendors might be happy to lend out their design team to you as well. After all, it is in the best interest of your vendors for you to get their product moving. If your display is going to focus on their product they will often be more than happy to help you create the best possible one. Not only that but they may provide you with posters and displays to help you both with window displays and displays inside of the store.

After all, merchandise is the centre point of any window display anyway. What's a window display for if not to sell merchandise as *well* as bring customers into your shop? Another thing you can do is lend out your window to local nonprofits. Being a part of the community is one of those things that helps you build relationships and connections with your customers. Doing such things turns you into a community leader—not just another retailer. It also is a good opportunity to get the press out to your store, which means pictures and free advertising when the article comes out.

Don't forget to walk around to other stores as well—you can take photographs of particularly great window displays. Lay them out and mark out what caught your eye about them and what they did right. When you come across a bad window display stop and figure out what they did wrong and why it was bad or uninspiring. Understanding what others have done right and wrong can be instrumental in helping you figure out what to do with your own windows.

You can also go all over the internet for pictures and ideas, as often people take pictures of window displays and post them up. The Google "images" section will give you a number of retail window displays pictures if you use "retail window display" as your search term keyword.

Window Displays

If you do feel a professional window display person is going to be the most cost effective idea for you, be sure to do the following:

- Check the portfolio to see if you are happy with the designs that the professional has done in the past.

- Check for references! This is one of the most important parts of your store. You cannot afford to hire someone who is going to leave the job unfinished. Both of these items are true for amateur artists that you might desire to hire as well.

- Put together a schedule for the work and understand exactly what will be done when.

- Sit down and discuss the display, the theme, your unique targeted customer and the needs of your shop with your designer so that you're both on the same page. See what ideas and creative thoughts your designer has for you.

- Some window displays won't focus on products at all, but on your store's brand—these are called brand awareness window displays. Make sure that whoever you are working with has a good understanding of your brand.

If at all possible, get recommendations from non-competing stores whose window designs you liked when you scouted out the local area.

Setting Up Shop

Window Displays for Drivers

Window displays should always appeal at the speed of the traffic you're trying to pull through your door. If the traffic passing by your store is primarily foot traffic then you should obviously create your display with foot traffic in mind. However, more and more anything anyone sees in a window display is going to happen from the window of a car.

For example, right away you know that any signage or lettering will have to be both increased in size and decreased in verbiage to appeal to any drivers making their way down your avenue. Longer signs with smaller letters will just get missed entirely. You might need a single word or two which can entice the driver to stop what she is doing, pull in, and park her car in your parking lot rather than continuing to drive on to whatever her original destination was.

If you're planning displays for drivers you also need to avoid motion displays wherever possible. Certain types of motion can be very distracting for drivers or difficult for them to process or understand quickly. Neither of these two things is very conducive to helping you get people to stop and park.

In point of fact everything has to be done a bit larger with the driver in mind. You literally need to go stand on the other side of the street to make sure whatever's in your window display is clear. You can't use neat smelling and sound tricks to do the job here. You have to really consider what's going to make it happen when the driver is zooming by. Knowing the speed limit on your particular street is going to be vital as well—window design for cars stuck in traffic going 10 miles per hour is going to be very different than window design for a 50 mile per hour busy street.

Window Displays

Your lighting will also need to account for factors like glare—at certain times of day your windows may be all but impossible to see unless you take steps to mitigate it. Timed lighting can change the lighting on your display to account for whatever the lighting conditions are outside. You'll also want to use bolder, darker, more dramatic colors to catch and hold the eye. Pale pastels won't get the driver's peripheral vision, and when you're trying to catch the attention of driver's you're certainly competing with a lot of important things, starting with all of the other drivers.

Once you've created your window display, have someone else drive by it themselves. It's best if they can work the drive into some other standard part of their day. If they can't remember the display when you ask them about it at the end of the day then you might not have created a very effective one. Ask your customers, too, as they surely see the display whether they originally intended to come in or not. Remember, if the display doesn't appeal to the unique targeted customer then something's wrong no matter what.

Above all, your window display should let the customer know they are welcome and that they'll be comfortable and happy once they come inside. If your window provides some diversion or amusement for a heavy traffic situation then you'll have the ability to bring new people through your door.

Effective Advertising

You cannot survive merely on your regular customers, drive-bys and walk-ins. Sooner or later it's going to become imperative for you to reach out to the rest of the city—and to do so in a way that entices those people to burn their very expensive gas to come and buy what you've got to offer.

Most people don't advertise at all effectively. They don't write good copy. They don't advertise enough or in the correct places. They don't take full advantage of all of the media available to them.

Once again you may indeed be cutting costs but this is NOT the place to start. Advertising is the only thing capable of keeping you alive in these competitive times. Your adverts should be like your window display—creative, seductive, and in possession of a clear call to action which brings people through the front door. Fail at any of these and all you have is the people who happen to walk by or drive by. Since fewer people are browsing when they shop at all, you may have a problem. You need to appeal to the people who show up at a store with a specific purpose, in need of a specific item.

These "seekers" are going to constitute 99% of your sales. People just do not have the time, energy, or patience to browse any longer. You need to literally reach out and grab them by the throat and drag them to your store while making them think it was their idea all along.

It takes being exposed to an ad roughly 9-10 times before that ad has a hope of succeeding. The first few times are just getting the name of the store to sort of lodge into the customer's head. You have to get name recognition before you ever get people through the door. Few people show up until they've got a compelling need some 10 impressions down the line. The only time this isn't true is when you're dealing with the Yellow Pages. People who open up the Yellow Pages are in search of someone who does what you do and so this ad can be handled somewhat differently— but in a fashion that takes full advantage of the reasons that people go to the Yellow Pages in the first place.

Effective Ad Design

When you design an ad you need to remember one key principle—pretty much right off the bat. Nobody cares what the name of your store is. Nobody cares what your phone number is and nobody cares what street you are on. None of that happens until you **make** them care. Until you've grabbed their attention so well that they seem to have no choice but to make the drive out and to come see.

Too many people kick off their ads with the name of their store as if the name of their store were the most important thing in the world. In truth, the name of the store can tell an awful lot about what the store is and does, and this is often what leads to the mistake. Most people are not professional copywriters and so they are forced to fall back on hit and miss tactics.

You need to kick off your ad with a compelling headline. Compelling headlines:

- Address the problem the customer may be facing. What problems does your merchandise solve? Why does your unique, targeted customer come in to buy your merchandise.

- Offers a deadline of some form or fashion. There's something pretty much universally true about the human race: we don't want to miss out. On anything. When faced with the possibility that someone might get something good that we will miss we tend to work a lot harder to get in on the opportunity.

- Asks a question. While not all headlines ask questions this is a great way to start. Advertising that focuses on "YOU", where "YOU" is the customer, will always do better than advertising that focuses on "WE", where "WE" is your retail store. Asking a question of the reader automatically turns the attention back on the customer in a very personal way that makes them think. Mentally, they stop to answer the question. As soon as they do so they are engaged with the ad.

Effective Advertising

After your headline you'll need a sub-headline. The sub-headline gives more information and adds additional reason to get where you want the customer to go. Keep the sub-headline aimed squarely at the customer.

After the sub-headline comes the body. The body will go over some benefits of the product. Bullet points are often easiest, but make sure you are giving benefits, not features. It can take a lifetime to get the difference between benefits and features: features are factual information about the product while benefits "paint the pictures."

- A feature of a bathing suit might be that it's one-piece. This is a *benefit* because you never have to worry about the bathing suit falling off at an embarrassing moment.

- A feature of a bakery is that it offers fresh bread. The *benefit* of the bakery is fresh, gourmet bread that you didn't have to make yourself.

- A feature of a bookstore is that it carries books. The *benefit* of a bookstore is all the latest titles, with expert, passionate readers to guide you to things you might love.

Whenever you find yourself trying to list out benefits you can use the features-benefits litmus test. Simply put, you can ask yourself, "Ok, so what does this *do?*" If you don't find the question clearly answered in whatever you just wrote down or typed then rewrite the sentence until you've got the answer staring you in the face.

One of the reasons people often have a problem with the whole features/benefits thing is that to them, the benefit seems obvious. We often get too close to our own stores and our own merchandise. We can't imagine how people can't see why they would need whatever it is just from the sheer fact of its existence and how cool it is. Sadly, people just don't think that way. Again, it takes awhile for those words to make their way through their brains in search of something to connect to. By the time they've made the connection and decided they might want whatever-it-is after all they're halfway down the road and the sale is lost.

You're taking away the work of painting the picture so that you make sure the customer gets it when and where you want them to get it—right around the time they remove the item from the rack and take it up to the front counter to pay for it.

It's only after your ad gets through these three items that you need to worry about including your personal information, your cool graphics, and directions to your store. At that point you've taken the steps that it takes for the customer to care.

All of this will require a little pre-writing on your part. Do you remember pre-writing? English teachers used to torment us with it when we were back in school. They sent us through strange, messy mind-maps or too-strict outlines. Well you're not going to do that sort of outline. You are, however, going to sit down and answer a series of questions before you try to compose your ad.

- What problems does our merchandise solve and for whom does our merchandise solve the problems?

- What makes our store different than every other store out there? Why should shoppers come see us over anyone else out there?

Effective Advertising

- What has our competition failed to do that we're doing?

- What are we failing to do that our competition has done? Be honest here—your competition will surely exploit your weaknesses. You have to be ready to answer this question head on.

- Who should see or hear my ad? Where can I go to reach this unique targeted customer?

- What is the tone that's most appropriate for my audience? Which words will appeal to them? As an example of how this works, think about the word "cool". You won't use "cool" the same way for a group of 20-30 year olds as you would for a group of 60-90 year olds. Understanding your audience is vital!!

- What are the benefits of my copy? How can I make sure those benefits aim straight to the heart of the customer while talking about the customer more than I talk about our store?

- Is there any jargon or are there any buzzwords related to my business? If so, list them out here— then make sure they don't ever appear in your ad.

- What will my specific call to action be? Ads are useless without a call to answer! Never leave it up to the customer to figure out what to do. Remember he or she is probably just scanning your ad. If you don't provide the call to action then people won't necessarily make the connection quickly enough to do what you want them to do.

- Are there any deadlines I can work into the ad? What can I do to create a sense of urgency? Remember that customers are acting on a sort of inertia. Any ad has to overcome the inertia of their daily routine so that they can get up and get out—to you.

- What testimonials or social proofs do I have access to? Have I won awards or recognition?

- Are there any promises I want to make that I can't deliver on? What promises can I deliver on—each and every time?

- What claims might I want to make that I'll be in a position of having to prove? Can they be proven?

A lot of people get very hung up on the ad design, but it's the wording of the ad that's important. It's the words that are going to entice the customer to act. Great design is of course very important—it can go extremely far in capturing attention and getting results. However, without the words your design isn't going to do very much.

You might have space or time concerns in your ad that you're going to have to pay attention to, so as you do this

Effective Advertising

"prewriting" exercise you should highlight the stuff that is the MOST important. That stuff should get in there first. In addition you never want to overwhelm the customer. Don't clutter up the space or fill a radio ad with so much information that nobody in their right mind could process it.

Avoid silly gimmicks—they won't help people make the decision to come to your store. You've probably seen or heard a number of silly gimmicks. Big chain retailers can afford to do weird stuff because they already have name brand recognition, but a small business like yourself does **not** have that luxury. Stick to the basics.

This is another arena where you might want to give some serious consideration to hiring a professional. Copywriters tend to work freelance and you might want to consider an affordable one. That said, with the understanding that budgets can be rather tight right now, it's not impossible for you to create the kind of copy you need to bring customers to your door.

Signage

There are a couple of different types of signs that you have to work with. There are, of course, the store signs that are outside of your building, but these signs have probably been in place for awhile and they aren't the kinds of signs that you need when it comes to bringing in more customers. Rather, you need to take a look at billboard or street signs.

Billboard advertising is actually remarkably effective, especially if you place your billboards about 15-20 minutes out from your store, then add them again at 5-10 minute intervals. This gets the customer thinking about coming into your store well before they have to turn off on the highway to get that done, and keeps reinforcing the idea till they find themselves taking the appropriate exit. Billboards are typically available at the rate of $400-$600/month.

You don't have as much space in the billboard to play around as you do with a longer print, radio, or television ad. You need bold colors. You need a "headline" that encompasses the benefits, because the headline and a quick set of directions to your store are about all you're going to get.

In order to create this headline you need to zero right in on the customer. Ask them a question. Talk to them. Let's take the clothing retailer with the new summer line. He might use something like:

| **Ready for summer yet?** |

If he adds his store name, a set of directions, and a high-impact graphic then he'll have an excellent sign which will bring people into his store.

"Series" billboards work very well too. These are billboards that build on one another as you make your way down the highway. They help to reinforce your message by pulling the customer in and keeping her entertained, instead of repeating the same tired message over and over and over again.

People see billboards all the time. They're effective, but if you can make them stand out in some way they'll be more effective. 3-D billboards which invoke more senses then the two dimensional sight can be exciting, effective ways to

Effective Advertising

advertise. Check out http://tinyurl.com/8nbary/ to see some truly cool billboards.

Your billboard advertising rep will have an art department you can take advantage of to help you, or you can go back to those art and graphic design students to get some low-cost help with your billboard. The billboard art department isn't always the best choice because they sometimes won't work as effectively for you. It's sad but true: your billboard rep wants your billboard to be just effective enough to be necessary but not so effective that you decide you don't really need the billboard anymore. Make sure you're really aware of the agenda of the people you work with.

Your vendors, too, can again help you with your billboards—but don't let one brand or vendor hijack your entire advertising campaign. You don't really want to be over-associated with one vendor or one brand, considering that if any of those brands run into trouble you're going to end up painted with the same brush if you do.

Point of Sale Advertising

Like point of sale displays, point of sale advertising carries some devastating effectiveness. Consider these coffee shop ads, available at http://tinyurl.com/42kq2j/.

Point of sale ads create an urgency to buy right at the places people go to buy, which is part of what makes them so helpful. You can use digital displays and rotate through several ads, but simple advertisements for various products that you wish to move can be really effective. Your vendors should have plenty of posters that you can use for point of sale advertising.

One of the reasons this advertising is so effective is the fact that customers are already in the "buying and paying" mindset while they're standing in line. The barriers that are normally there have already dropped. Even if the Pops advertising doesn't create an instant sale on the spot it can lodge the brand or message in the customer's subconscious, ready to be released later.

Point of sale displays can also be used to up sell or create add-on sales. Let's take a look at the baker, for example. You're sitting there selling bread and you also have cheese in your bakery. As the customer buys the bread a digital display shows off the perfect cheese paired with the bread you just rang up. More often than not the customer is going to suddenly decide she wants or need some cheese and ask for some. It's a process that happens at the speed of thought.

Obviously if the customer doesn't have enough money for cheese, or is really adverse to cheese, this isn't going to work. However chances are the cheese is going to enhance the customer's experience of the bread. So you've achieved multiple ends here. Increasing the amount of money a customer spends per visit is a much more cost-effective way to increase your bottom line than going after new customers. You have to do both of course—there's always a form of customer attrition that happens—but making the most of the customers you have is a strategy you shouldn't ignore. Consider this: if you get just 10 customers per day to spend $5 per visit on a 260 day work year, you'll have increased your store's revenue by $13,000 for the year. Point of sale advertising can help you achieve that vital end.

Make sure your point of sale content is extremely relevant to your customers or the ads won't do a lot of good. That's one reason why the digital displays that link up to the scanner are so popular—they ensure the products that flash before the customer's eyes are relevant to whatever else the customer is buying. If all you can manage is a poster, however, make sure to keep it relevant. If you're in a dress shop, focus on accessories at the point of sale. If you're in a bookshop, focus on bookmarks and book lights. Small "upsale" items work best at the point of sale, not big items that the customer will have to race back through the store for. If the point of sale ad works hand and hand with the point of sale merchandise display then you'll be ahead of the game.

It is illegal to market some products at the point of sale. For example, you're not allowed to market tobacco products at the point of sale. Most products won't have that issue but make sure you research any potentially controversial product just in case. You don't want to find out after you've already invested in the ad.

Make sure you train your counter staff on selling the product you plan to advertise at the point of sale. If customers are going to ask questions about the product they're going to do it right there—you don't want your associates caught in the position of having to say, "oh, er, I don't know," when an interested customer makes an inquiry. You'll lose the sale right then and there.

Another outstanding form of point of sale advertising happens when the receipt is printed out. Because UPC codes have made it so much easier to track everything some sales machines are capable of printing out relevant vendor coupons right at the register. Handing the customer a coupon for her favorite make-up because she happened to buy that very same brand is an excellent way of keeping yourself in the forefront of the customer's mind after she leaves the store. What's funny is you may never see the coupon again. It's likely to get lost or left unused—

but the customer will surely remember receiving it. Even if she does have it, since she could only use it in your store it got her back through your doors to buy something she enjoyed, and what could be a greater victory than that?

Local Press and Radio

Local press and radio are still very effective forms of advertising. However, you have to make sure to use these media correctly. Too often retailers (and any other advertiser) blow this medium by spending all of their money on one huge full color ad or radio blitz that runs for a single day. This is terribly ineffective because it takes all those multiple impressions for any ad to make an impact.

Your ad should run at least 8-10 weeks in the same spot and on a consistent basis to be effective. In addition you need to consider demographics. If your target customer is a college kid they are unlikely to go looking in the print newspaper for anything at all. They'll look on the internet—hands down. You might catch them on the radio but they're just as likely to be plugged into their MP3s. Use press and radio advertising only when you are really certain that your unique targeted customer reads the publication in question.

To find out what your customers are reading or listening to simply do an informal survey of favorite publications and radio stations. Like attracts like—if you have 20 customers who listen to WKPZ Radio 94.1, then chances are the rest of your target customers will also listen to WKPZ Radio 94.1. That makes the radio station a good bet—and with many radio stations to choose from you want to be sure to choose the station that's going to have the highest possible number of your target customers inside of it.

Effective Advertising

That said, you should *always* have a yellow pages ad, not just a listing, no matter who your target customer is. Even a 20 year old will look in the good old fashioned phone book occasionally. Besides, buying an ad in the yellow pages often comes with an internet option as well. Take advantage of both. Most people who go to the phone directory go knowing what they need but not WHO they need. They're in the buying mood and it's the perfect time to capture a customer. If you don't have one of these types of ads you're shooting yourself in the foot.

Make use of color in print ads, whether in the Yellow Pages or in the paper. Color can help make you stand out. That said spot color is often as effective as full color and it is certainly less expensive. Whatever you do, stay consistent—don't switch sections, don't switch sizes.

It's a good idea to use the newspaper or some other medium to test out ads that you might run in media with longer life cycles, like the Yellow Pages. Run a split A/B test in two separate publications and use two separate phone numbers to track the response. Use the ad that created the best response in the Yellow Pages. You can't change that ad for a whole year so you want your best possible ad.

That said, run your print and radio ad in 8-10 week cycles. Leave your ads alone without changing them during that time period, because the truth is you won't *know* how effective that ad is until you've allowed the proper life cycle.

Never rely on your newspaper or radio to write the ad for you. All too often you'll end up with the sales rep trying to write the ad for you. The rep wants your next order, which means they want the ad to be just effective enough but not so effective that they don't need you anymore. Or the rep will just be too inexperienced with writing good ads to know what he or she is doing. These are sales people— even if their business cards say they are "ad consultants."

What are the "ad consultants" relying on? Simply this: they're relying on the fact that the mere repetition of "impressions" will actually get a few people in the door. No matter how bad your ad, if you flash it at enough people enough times you'll see some results. That said you don't want to be in the position of investing a whole lot of money into a bad ad!

Good radio ads don't even bother with phone numbers, items, or prices. This isn't information the average listener retains. You can deal with all of that in a print ad because the reader has the ability to rip the ad out of whatever publication you're dealing with and take it with him or her. The radio listener is most likely to be in his or her *car*. She is not stopping to jot down the number or the prices. She's half listening to you. Therefore you want a message that's simple, that's repetitive, and that's capable of sticking in the mind while creating a compelling reason to come down and see more.

Since you're focused on getting people in the door you might want to focus on landmark directions. For example, a good radio ad might go something like this:

The new summer clothing line is ready for you at Steve's. Exit 39 off Hwy 59, across from the Meijer. Get ready for summer! Exit 39 off Hwy 59, across from Meijer.

These words are easy to remember. They tell people why they need to come and they tell people how to get there. Once the customer has heard those same things over and over again they're likely to respond to them. It doesn't require them to remember more than where to go and what to get when they go there. Radio ads aren't long lists of benefits—they're simply programming that you're inserting into the minds of the people listening.

Avoid talking heads or stilted dialogue. Avoid weird jingles. These things mostly just serve to make your business look silly. The entire purpose of a radio ad is to get people in the door, not really to get them focused on buying. You can get them zeroed in on buying once they are there.

Websites can make your radio ads very effective—people can often remember websites with far greater clarity than they can remember phone numbers. This is also true for print ads—people often want to go to websites these days to check it out. Your store should already have a website, but if it does not you **almost have to invest in one.** There are far more reasons than your radio and print ad spots to take care of this detail, but if you haven't done it yet, now is the time.

Remember that in any advertising medium you have seconds, not minutes, to capture attention and provide a compelling reason to act on the ad. Write any kind of advertisement with that fact firmly in your head.

Word of Mouth

Even in this high tech era, word-of-mouth advertising still works. You want and need to do everything in your power to foster it. Word of mouth advertising is the most powerful form of advertising, both because it costs you nothing and because people are more inclined to believe their friends and family than they are *you.*

Setting Up Shop

The only way to create word of mouth advertising is by going above and beyond the customer's expectation: each and every time. You need your customers *raving* about what a great thing doing business with you is!

The only sure way to ensure this is through the creation of processes. Processes, checklists, and procedures ensure that the right things happen whether the staff is having a good day or a bad day. It makes sure that everyone in the store knows how to help the customer and knows how to "own" the situation. You want to get beyond the personality foibles of the staff having an impact on the smooth operation of your store.

The little extras you work in—things you give away at each visit, for example—should never get mentioned in your primary advertising. The idea is to create a little "surprise" experience that customers will remember and talk about them. So if you give away a free petit fours at every visit your customers shouldn't know that till they get there.

You can also create events—known as event marketing—to generate word of mouth advertising. People will come to the event and tell other people about it. Event marketing, from contests to picnics, takes a bit of creativity and planning. That said it can be *well* worth it in terms of generating "buzz" about your store.

You can also make sure that your employees are fully trained before you get them on the floor or on a register. Get them working on a dummy register or something before you toss them into the line of fire so that you don't end up with the newbie trying to fumble through serving an increasingly angry customer. The smoother and more professional the customer's experience the more likely it will be that the customer will both come back *and* recommend your business to a friend.

Effective Advertising

All those procedures help create a very consistent experience for your customer. Customers tend to return to places they like because they want to have the same experience over again. If you handle things haphazardly, in a "take it as it comes" fashion, you will never manage to create such an experience.

Building those relationships—the way we discussed in Chapter 1—is also a way to help ensure that you get the word of mouth advertising that you so desperately need.

The Internet

The internet is sort of a strange duck for high street retailers. It is a competitor. It is a tool. It is something which helps build relationships and it's something which puts a world of distance between ourselves and our customers.

All the same, you **must** have a website. You can get someone to do a website for you professionally, or you can get an inexpensive "drag and drop" website like what's available at www.vistaprint.com. I'd recommend a professional though, simply because creating something attractive to convey your brand is so vital. You also need to have enough traffic to make the website go.

That said the way you handle your website is just not going to be the same that most "internet marketers" are handling it. You're not really out to generate millions of hits to your site every day, particularly if you operate in a smaller town. You want the people who live in your geographic area to check out your website—you hardly care about anyone else. You might get lucky and sell something via your online shopping cart but for the most part your aim is to have a place to market your store to the local community.

When you have a high street website you're using it for a couple of things:

- To give people a place to go check you out online so they can decide whether to visit or not. This will include information about your store and your products. It will also include a map to your store and contact information.

- A place to put in customer service requests or special orders of any form. Getting some of your customer service to e-mail can prevent some nasty scenes in the front of your store while other people are trying to shop.

- A place to send people when you only have a few seconds to tell them anything about your store.

- A place to send people to your social media, such as Twitter or Facebook.

- A place to build up your store's mailing list. Even a small town store can benefit from some sort of e-mail newsletter. You can use an ESP geared towards the small shop, like Constant Contact, but it's always good to stay a part of your customer's world.

Effective Advertising

Getting involved with internet social media can be even more helpful to your shop than having a website. Be sure to check out all the ways you can use Twitter and Facebook to create a business network for yourself and to drive sales. You can use both to make you more personable as well as to keep you right in the forefront of the customer's mind. Many of your customers can be found on both social networking forums.

You also need to use things like Google Local to list your business. Paid listings on Yahoo are not a bad idea either. Neither is PPC advertising if you bid on local keywords like, "Peoria, IL bakery" or "Evansville, IL summer clothes." Don't worry about more generalized keywords because again, you want to make sure you drive traffic from the local area.

PPC Advertising, stands for pay-per-click, which means that you only pay when someone actively clicks on your advertisement. Because you're using such a specialized keyword you are unlikely to pay more than five or six cents per click. This can be a very cost effective way to get advertising done. Check out PPC programs at Google, Yahoo, and Bing.com as each one of them is set up a little bit differently. There is also a PPC Facebook. With some of these programs you can target the PPC ads to only show up to a certain demographic in a certain geographic area— which means you can declare who your unique targeted customer is and set your online advertising to the task of reaching out to them.

Craigslist ads are free, and you can also use Craigslist to get people both to your website and to the door of your store. Don't forget, as well, that with the economic crash most newspapers have moved online. Any effective newspaper advertising in many areas of the world is going to rely solely on having a website to visit when someone happens along and clicks on the link in question. If you rely on the ad and the ad alone you're essentially going to shoot yourself in the foot.

The major reason you're going to want to advertise on the internet is the simple fact that most people research products online before they decide to go out and make any purchases. If you're not online, even if your primary business is done on the streets, you will appear backwards and behind the times. That's probably not the image you want to convey. Some members of the younger generation will not even work with you if you don't have a website!

Seasonal Sales and Discounting

Seasonal sales and discounts can be great ways to bring customers through your door. They take advantage of times when people are typically shopping anyway and use that need to bring in the foot traffic. Yet there are pitfalls associated with seasonal sales that you should be aware of. For example you don't want to try to target every single season in terms of sales and discounts. If your store is constantly discounting then you're going to manage to label yourself as a "discount store." This is not often the image most high street retailers really want to convey.

In addition, discounting too much, or at the wrong times, can really and truly shoot you and the bottom line right in the foot just for the simple fact that you're giving away the farm too often. Seasonal sales are absolutely a strategy that you are going to be adopting and using to your advantage.

Seasonal sales can be a double edged sword because we often hire more staff during a busy season as well. If we're not careful we can find ourselves slashing prices at the exact same time that we hire new associates.

All too often retailers are attempting to sell on price when they should be selling on anything else. You should actually stop and evaluate whether or not you want to do anything seasonal to begin with. If you're selling on quality, customer service, or any form of uniqueness then you might not wish to damage your brand with clearance prices—even at the heart and height of Christmas holiday.

Besides, you ought to consider off-season discounts at least as strongly as you consider seasonal discounts. Consider this: on any kind of season your customers basically *have* to shop. They aren't going to get around getting Christmas presents for their family, for example. Sales can carry you through the points and times when you *don't* have to shop at all.

You also have to decide how much of your store is going to participate in the season at all. This is not such a cut and dried decision as you might think.

The Seasonal Options

First, are you intending to turn your whole store to the task of "getting seasonal" or are you going to simply leave getting seasonal to a single, dedicated aisle in the store? Will the seasonal theme hit your window display or will it be understated? Are you going to discount things leading up to the season or are you going to wait and discount them later? Which seasons will your store even honor, and, more importantly, *why* will your store honor them?

A lot of retailers start discounting and doing sales like crazy during their chosen seasons. Others have found they've done really well by raising prices! Not only does a higher price convey the idea that something is more valuable than a lower price does, but it also helps to give you more money for the same amount of work.

That said, most shops *do* engage in some sort of seasonal sale. So the trick here is understanding your options and figuring out the options that are going to contribute the most to drawing in your unique, targeted customers.

A lot of retailers go a little crazy over seasonal issues. However seasons won't save your store if you're having trouble. Before you start resorting to seasonal sales and gimmicks you need to make sure all the other marketing elements of your store are in place. Seasonal discounts need to be an enhancement to the process, not a placebo pill to shore up a dying venture.

Among the options for the seasons are in choosing the right seasons for your store. In doing so, you should ask yourself:

- What seasons are likely to be important to my Unique Targeted Customer, and why?

- What seasons do my customers *expect* the store to get involved in?

- How can we make the season special for the customer here at the store? Does making the season special involve discounts or sales or is there another direction we can take our promotions or presentation in?

- What window displays have I planned? These displays should create a beginning blueprint for other seasonal activities in your store.

- Do I want to have sales that don't have anything to do with a specific holiday or time of year? Why don't I want to have them?

- Are my vendors coming out with any hot new products this year? If so should I treat any of these product launches like my own "season?"

- If I discount, to what extent will I do so?

- If I hire additional staff for the season, to what extent will I do so?

- Can I create my own seasons through use of special events, drawings, product giveaways and classes that help me teach people new skills to use with the merchandise I sell?

Once you've planned all these factors you will have a full scale seasonal strategy in front of you, awaiting deployment. Note, as well, that discounting is not *always* a bad thing and the season can give you an excuse that doesn't make you look desperate. We all end up with stale product sometimes: product that isn't performing at all or performing to par.

Seasonal Sales and Discounting

Seasonal Market Research

People don't shop the same way during a seasonal period. People don't even shop the same way across different seasons. It's important to do your market research for each season so you don't waste time or money.

Some of this will start by researching the competition and what the competition plans to do for the season. Your eye should always be turned towards making yourself more competitive, which invariably means watching and understanding what the other guy might be doing.

Knowing when your store's "rush periods" are likely to be can be a major factor in determining staffing needs, inventory needs, and advertising needs. A flower shop is going to have an entirely different "rush period" than a craft store. Toy stores will absolutely see a sharp increase in sales between Thanksgiving and Christmas. You need to research when the customers are most likely to come in and drop a lot of money if you want to make the most of the situation.

Remember, too, that it's not just your store that experiences seasonal ups and downs. Your vendors should be able to show exact figures on how their product has performed in other, similar stores across various seasons. You need to have a good idea of what product to purchase and stock up into your store. You can't do that without any solid data about the situation. Chocolate mints, for example, do best between the months of October-December.

Seasons can be a great time to launch new product. You can do market research on the type of product in general to find out when sales are likely to spike for those products and introduce the product in the proper time to make sure that it creates a maximum impact. Don't ignore the vendor's own marketing strategy. HD TVs, for example, received huge amounts of "hype" when they first came out. It would have been a mistake to ignore that hype instead of riding the high of it.

You should also research the impact of starting seasons on your customers. Some customers, for example, get very disgusted to see Christmas stuff put out in October. This immediately makes them feel stressed out, pressured, harried and over-commercialized.

Others are just happy for the reminder that Christmas shopping isn't really all *that* far away and will start buying some of their presents early. Where does your UTC fall on *that* particular scale? All you can do is ask.

By gauging the demand for certain traditional seasonal items each and every season you can avoid making costly purchasing mistakes that will haunt you for the rest of the year. Season-specific items which can only be sold at certain times of the year can be dangerous simply because you are stuck with anything you can't get rid of at the end of the season. You either have to sell it at a loss after the season is complete or hold onto it on the hopes of moving the stale old product off the shelf at the beginning of the next season. Neither of these two options is particularly conducive to a happy bottom line.

Often your seasonal strategy will be a total-store affair. That is, there's not going to be a single shelf or department that gets away from the seasonal strategy. This is going to require a lot of advance work on your part, meaning you should be planning each season 3-4 months in advance of the season. This not only includes merchandising and sales but also includes merchandising displays and window displays. It encompasses any special marketing you feel you might have to do to make the absolute most out of the season.

The Seasonal Aisle

Your market research may reveal that there's no need to deal with seasons at all, or that the season won't be nearly so profitable as you might wish. Yet you might still feel culturally obligated to do *something* seasonal in your store when certain seasons arise. You may find you have a percentage of customers that really does like going seasonal even if everybody else on your customer list doesn't.

The seasonal aisle can be a great happy medium. It can keep you from spending more money than you want to spend. Instead of dealing with entire store overhauls for a variety of seasons you can simply devote a single aisle— usually out at the front of the store—to whatever the seasonal item or items are. This can work well, too, for seasonal items that you *need* to sell seasonally but which do not appeal to every customer that walks into your door.

Take an office supply store for example. Part of your customer base is sure to have kids. This means "Back to School," but not every person who walks back into your door cares about Back to School. Some of them are just trying to get a printer cartridge for the office fax machine and might well find themselves annoyed to see the entire store transformed into kiddie-land. Yet if you don't appeal to that secondary UTC you'll lose a huge amount of money that you could have gotten through taking advantage of the season.

Setting Up Shop

This is the perfect time, then, to devote an aisle or two to the Back to School season while allowing the remainder of your store to focus on the high end corporate customer that is your primary UTC. You don't lose any opportunities this way.

The seasonal aisle should usually be near the front end of the store, right within sight. This can have the effect of giving your store some seasonal personality as well as helping people to understand that you do have the seasonal items.

The seasonal aisle is almost it's very own form of special retail display. The thing about having this aisle ready and good to go is that you can go ahead and just designate it for all of your seasonal things. You can of course integrate the display into the store when you do a total-store season promotion, but for the seasons where you've decided a partial seasonal aisle is your best bet it is there to be changed out with fresh product geared towards the time of year.

You often do not have to discount anything at all in the seasonal aisle. You are probably aware that most people believe anything in a special display is, in fact, on sale—even if there is no other evidence about to support that fact at all. In fact, adding discounts at this phase can call attention to everything else that isn't discounted and be counterproductive to moving the product.

It can be a good idea to keep your seasonal aisle—and everything seasonal—in your store somewhat understated. Many, many people have grown quite weary with the "seasonal assault" – the sudden slam of holiday music, holiday decorations, themed holiday products and holiday greetings that seems to leap out at people from every spare corner of every spare shelf. You can actually stand *out* by *toning it down.* This is *especially* true if you cater to a high end, high class, high dollar clientele. Coming across like a cheesy discount bargain store with a dozen plastic Santas leering down from every corner is *not* the image your UTC is going to enjoy. Use your seasonal aisle to create the best of both worlds, so to speak.

Seasonal Discount Strategies

You may have been conditioned, a bit, by your own retail shopping. Part of your brain has been programmed to think Christmas (or many other seasons, for that matter) is a time for great discounts. Therefore you might be tempted to run around your own establishment discounting everything in sight, simply because you fear it might not get bought otherwise.

This is the time to stop and think very carefully. You've got to get moving with a strategy or you're going to discount yourself into a loss—and you might not even have to.

- Should you discount during the season at all? Some retailers believe that you should only discount after the season is done. Why? Because people have to buy during the season. They might not have to buy from *you,* but they have to buy. The theory is, if you have the right Christmas present then people are going to buy that present regardless of whether it's on sale or not. Therefore, putting that product on sale amounts to little more than shooting yourself in the foot.

- Other schools of thought believe that people will constantly use this time of year to go searching for the best bargain and will pass you buy if they don't see it. They believe that the customer feels more or less *entitled* to the right bargain. These retailers tend to mark up their prices quite a bit more during the non-seasonal portion of the year in order to absorb the "sale" at the seasonal portion of the year. They do not simply discount their stuff.

- Some of your vendors might not allow you to discount their products at all—or they might not allow you to discount very much. This can be for reasons of image and brand management, or it could be part of their business strategy. Some might allow markdowns but only to a certain threshold of basic price floor. So you'll either have to again, mark up the price during the rest of the year to absorb the "sale" later or you'll have to avoid selling those products at retail—which can leave you with those products sitting on your sales floor: stale and unmoving.

- Loss leaders can become very advantageous if you use the right loss leaders. For example, during the Christmas season you might discount wine or chocolates very heavily—and then strategically place a whole host of other non-discounted product around the store. You win if the sale item causes people to continue around the store and buy a whole host of other things at full price. You lose if all they do is come in to buy the discount candy.

Seasonal Sales and Discounting

- Multiple buys can be a good way to shield yourself from the impact of bad discounting. For example you can offer a percentage discount on one product after the customer has bought a second version of the same product at regular price. You move more merchandise and increase your profits this way, and you keep yourself from falling into the dangerous "discounting rut."

- Appeal to speed shoppers! Put your "discounted" merchandise on the highest and lowest shelves and keep your regular priced merchandise up at eye level. A lot of people come zooming through the stores right around the holidays. They may be drawn by the sale sign but then just want to get in and get out. So they don't look for the bargains, they shop in a hurry, and they walk out spending money thinking they saved it. In the meantime, you win.

Seasonal Packaging Strategies

You may not have a whole lot of control over the way your vendors package things—but you have total control over your interior store signage and arrangement. Think of the more stressful shopping times of the year—again Christmas comes to mind as the easiest example. People are going crazy trying to get a multitude of gifts. Anything you can do to help them along and make quick decisions has two effects:

- It puts money in your pocket.

- It actually engenders a feeling of gratitude in the overstressed customer who had some of the work of actually thinking about all these matters taken right off of her chests.

For the holiday season you can arrange your aisles, shelves, and displays in categories that actually tell your customers who to buy what for. Consider:

- For Dad.

- For Mom.

- For the Kids.

- For the Husband.

- For the Wife.

- For the Golf Lover.

- For the Chocolate Lover.

- For the Animal Lover.

People know these things (chocolate lover, animal lover) about their loved ones without necessarily being completely sure what these people actually *want* in terms of gifts. You are practically telling these people what to buy if you handle your merchandising in this way during the seasons. This strategy is the most effective when you're doing a total-store season strategy.

Gift baskets, gift cards at the register, and other "quick gift" items can be exceptional items to have on hand during any season. They're good for impulse purchases, displays, and other items that are just kind of picked up in passing. Smaller items, more generic items that people keep on hand to give out as gifts, are excellent as well.

Make sure you offer gift wrapping during any holiday season. Gift wrapping makes great marketing, because you will always have the name of your store somewhere in or on the gift wrap. Thus you create almost a "viral" marketing tool that ends up handed off to the gift's recipient just as soon as the gift leaves the hands of the giver.

Retail is challenging during the best of times—and at any season of the year. Yet with enough attention to detail you can supercharge your marketing and become even stronger during a weak economy. Let the weak economy weed out your competition while you rise to the challenge of marketing your business to the very best of your ability. Don't ever let yourself become frazzled—not in any season. Concentrate, instead, on paying close attention to your customers. Concentrate on offering the best experience you possibly can. Your sales will increase!